SUNDULOS

AN INVITATION TO SERVICE

WRITTEN BY: C.D. McNEILL

ILLUSTRATED BY: HAILEY CAMPBELL

TextTalk
Media Ministries, LLC

SUNDULOS
An Invitation to Service

Table of Contents

INTRO

What does it mean to serve, how should I serve, and who is rewarded from my work?? Jesus teaches that the greatest among His people is a servant. The driving force of this guidebook is to find and nurture that spirit in young men who are working or preparing for work in the Lord's kingdom, which is His church.

That's right; helping others with what they need to worship God in spirit and in truth is a job! Are you the guy that God is looking for? Do you have what it takes to be a worker in the Lord's church? What if you could be hired to serve in God's house? Guess what, you can!

Matthew 20:1-16

shows Jesus' teaching about the church and its workers in a parable about a vineyard.

There was work available for those who wanted to work. Although the workers were hired at different times of the day, everyone was rewarded fairly.

When someone wants a job, they apply for it. They know that the job is available because the company has advertised the position they want to fill. Important positions in the working world are agreed upon every day, like the Rescue Squad and Sanitation workers. It's amazing how the skills needed for different jobs end up working together to serve the needs of people.

Back in the day, people would look in the newspaper, go to the unemployment office, or ask someone who had a job they were interested in, if they were hiring. Today people mostly go online to search for work.

Let's look at the job listings, that's right, the advertisement for positions in the Lord's church.

Where do you think we should look if we want to work for Christ? If you said the Bible, you're one step closer to being a servant in the kingdom.

Every act of worship, and the people needed
to carry it out are founded in the gospel
of Christ.

EPHESIANS 4 speaks of the gifts of God given to
all mankind (which includes women).

EPHESIANS 4:11-12 Now these are the gifts
Christ gave to the church: the apostles, the
prophets, the evangelists, and the pastors and
teachers. Their responsibility is to equip God's
people to do his work and build up the church,
the body of Christ.

ACTS 6:3 The Apostles gave instruction to select
faithful men to make sure certain widows were
not left hungry.

These are all great jobs in the church that
continually need to be filled, except for
Apostles and prophets. Their work has already
been done.

There's a lot of serving happening in the kingdom of Christ, but don't worry, you will get the best training to make useful the abilities you have now.

What is the job for you? To begin, let's focus on some works that take place during the worship service.

There's singing, praying, and communion along with a few other tasks that the saints of God must complete each time they gather for worship.

Our service is not only needed on the first day of the week, but every day in the life of a Christian.

Before we dive into serving the Lord's church, let's notice who were called on to carry out various ministries.

Section Assessment

1. **HOW MANY** men were selected to serve the widows in **ACTS 6?**

WHAT were their **NAMES?**

2. **WHAT** causes works and worship to be in **VAIN?**

3. **WHO** should good works in Christ **GLORIFY?**

MINISTRIES FOR ME

You may be wondering, or already have an idea of where you can best serve when the family of God gathers. We notice a pattern on the first day of the week (Sunday), when the disciples came together to worship.

ACTS/WORKS OF WORSHIP

THEY SANG .... EPHESIANS 5:19

THEY PRAYED .... 1 THESSALONIANS 5:17

THEY GAVE .... 2 CORINTHIANS 9:7

THERE WAS PREACHING .... ACTS 20:7

THEY BROKE BREAD .... 1 CORINTHIANS 11:23

They communed or
commemorated Christ
with unleavened bread
and the fruit of the vine
(grape juice) which
represented the body
and blood of Christ who
was slain for the sin of all humanity.

I bet you can perform one of the above tasks.
You may possess the ability to do them all.
Rest assured, there will be times you are
needed to serve when you don't believe you
are the best to serve the need. Yessir, a need!!
A true servant will on many occasions have to
deny their own comfort to serve others.

Do you still have a desire to serve? Alright!
Let's get dressed up for work.

Section Assessment

1. What are the **ACTS/WORKS OF WORSHIP** found in the New Testament church?

2. What kind of **GIVER** does God love?

3. **WHEN** did Paul finish preaching?
Have you ever been told to dress for the job?

All Dressed Up

Since this is spiritual work, you're going to need spiritual clothing. Being dressed simply means you have put something on.

GALATIANS 3:27 says, "For as many of you (true Christians) as have been baptized into Christ have put on Christ." Just as God made clothing to cover Adam and Eve, we need to be covered in Christ before we begin our labor. Once covered, we must commit to and continue good works in the Lord. **(1 CORINTHIANS 15:58)**

Section Assessment

1. **WHAT** must I **PUT ON** before I serve Christ?

2. Is it possible for **HARD WORK** and **DEDICATION** in the Lord's church to go **UNNOTICED?**

MY WORK ETHIC

LET'S SEE HOW THEY DID IT

COLOSSIANS 3:23-24 says, "Work willingly at whatever you do, as though you were working for the Lord rather than for people. 24 Remember that the Lord will give you an inheritance as your reward, and that the Master you are serving is Christ."

The word of God is always true, and so is the verse above. The men who led the early church had to obey God and be willing to serve Him. That's the attitude we should remember to have when there is work to be done. Have you ever heard of the prophet who told God, "Here am I, send me."?

WORK means to put something in motion.

WORK ETHIC is an attitude of determination and dedication toward one's job.

God is Spirit, but He decided for us to be flesh and bones. That's not all! He also gave us His spirit. This helps us to know that working for God will utilize physical ability for a spiritual purpose. The spirit that every man has is the spirit of life, but there is a special spirit we must have to serve the Lord. That spirit is the Holy Spirit!

When we are a part of the Lord's workforce the spirit helps us to get work done. This process starts in our mind when we let the word sink in and lead us.

My young brother and friend, God wants you to work for Him. Remember, no man, not even a young man, can serve two masters. If you have a heart of service, I encourage you to use it to serve God in His kingdom. He will make sure you have everything that you need.

Now may the God of peace—who brought up from the dead our Lord Jesus, the great Shepherd of the sheep, and ratified an eternal covenant with His blood—may He equip you with all you need for doing His will. May He produce in you, through the power of Jesus Christ, every good thing that is pleasing to Him. All glory to Him forever and ever! Amen.

HEBREWS 13:20–21

ONE LAST QUESTION:

Is there something in you that desires to be my fellow worker in the churches of Christ?

(ROMANS 16:16)

Candidates for Hire

In **Acts 6:3**, we see baptized brothers being instructed by the Apostles to select seven men from the congregation to serve Gentile widows in need. They were to be full of the spirit, which comes in baptism, and be wise. Once the congregation chose men of right faith, they were brought back to the spiritual leaders (the Apostles), who prayed and laid hands on them.

This shows that the servants did not serve in a manner separate from the teaching that had been handed down from Christ once and for all.

Technically, any living soul is a candidate to serve in the Lord's kingdom; but so many disqualify themselves when they deny the commandments given by Jesus.

(Mark 7:7-9)

Yes, if you are willing to hear and obey Christ, you are on your way to many great works as a servant in the Lord's church. Being out front while serving the people of God, those in the community, and possibly internationally will shine a lot of light on you. Yep, people will notice your works, and sometimes give you a little praise.

NEVER forget, you are a light for Christ, and your work must glorify the Father in Heaven! (MATTHEW 5:16)

Now we can do all things through Christ which strengthens us.

Have you been thinking about the work that you desire to do?

David said, "I was glad when they said unto me, let us go to the house of the Lord".

I wonder if he just wanted to go, or if he wanted to be useful when he got there?

Section Assessment

1. Define **WORK** in your own words.

2. **WHO** was glad to go to the **HOUSE OF THE LORD?**

(Bonus: support your answer with Scripture.)

3. **WHAT** is **WORK ETHIC?**